Mandala Wonders

ANIMALS WILDLIFE

For beginners

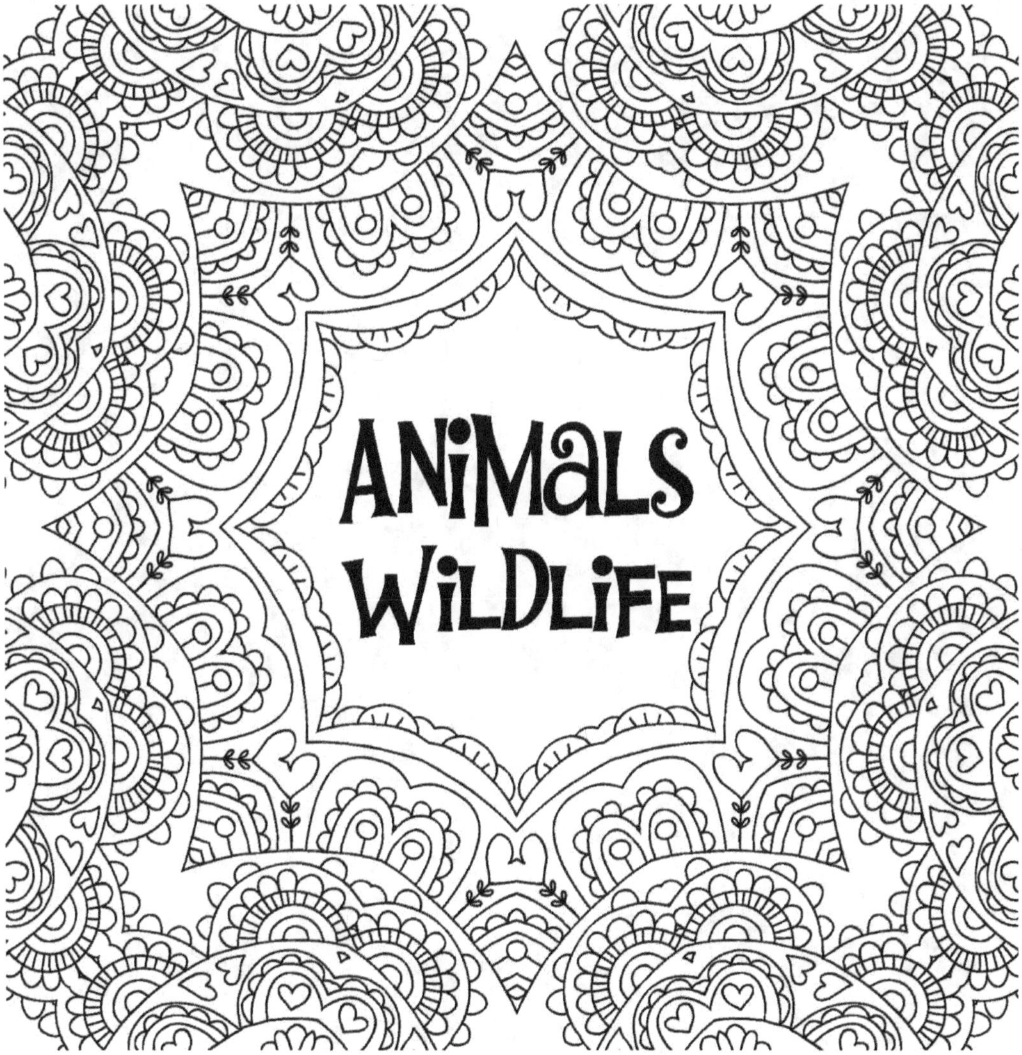

ANIMALS WILDLIFE

Almond Vinnie

Mandala Wonders

ANiMals WiLDLife

For beginners

ISBN-13:978-1536826302
ISBN-10: 1536826308

Deer

Bison

Antilope

Bear

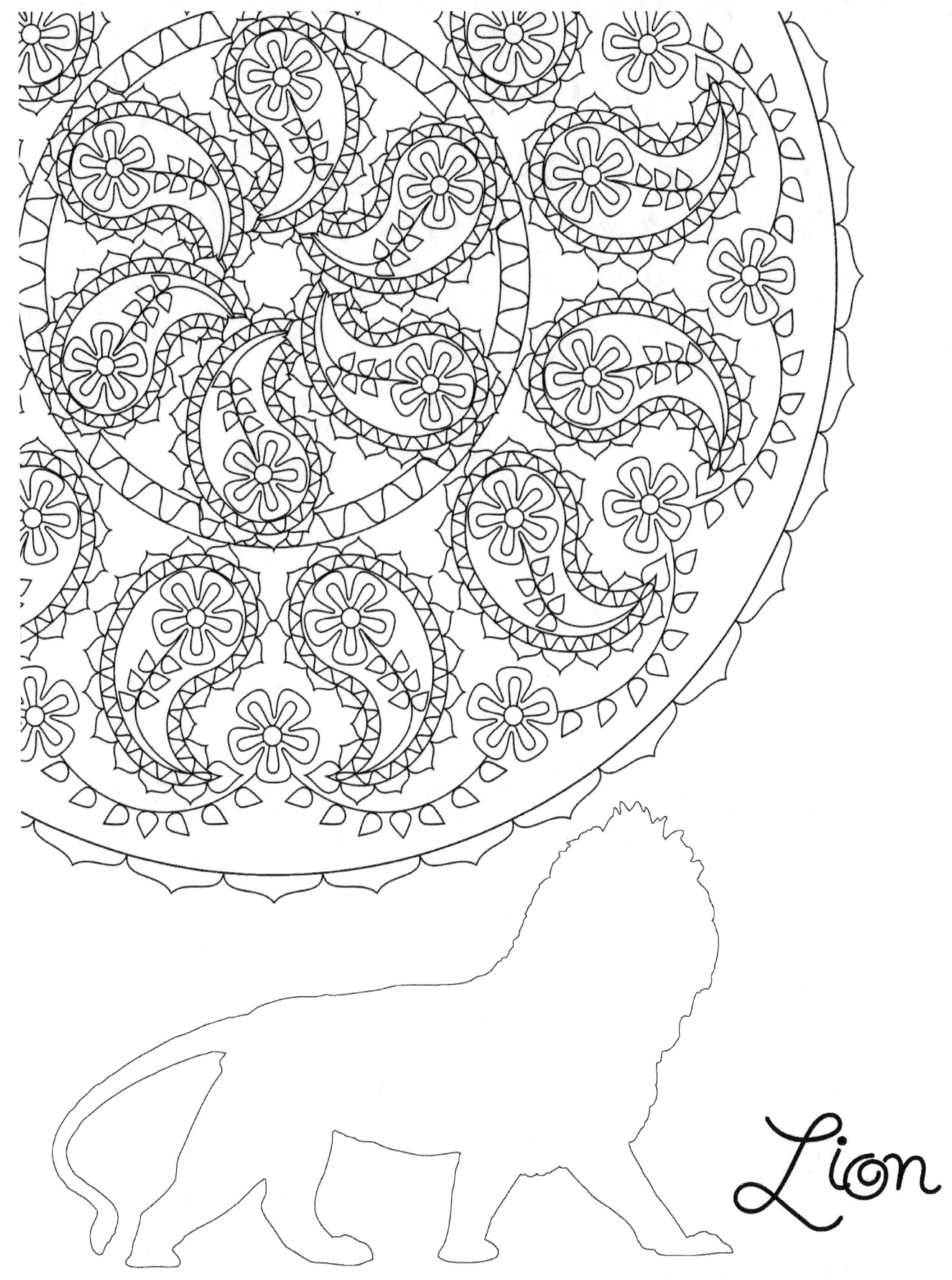

Lion

Mammut

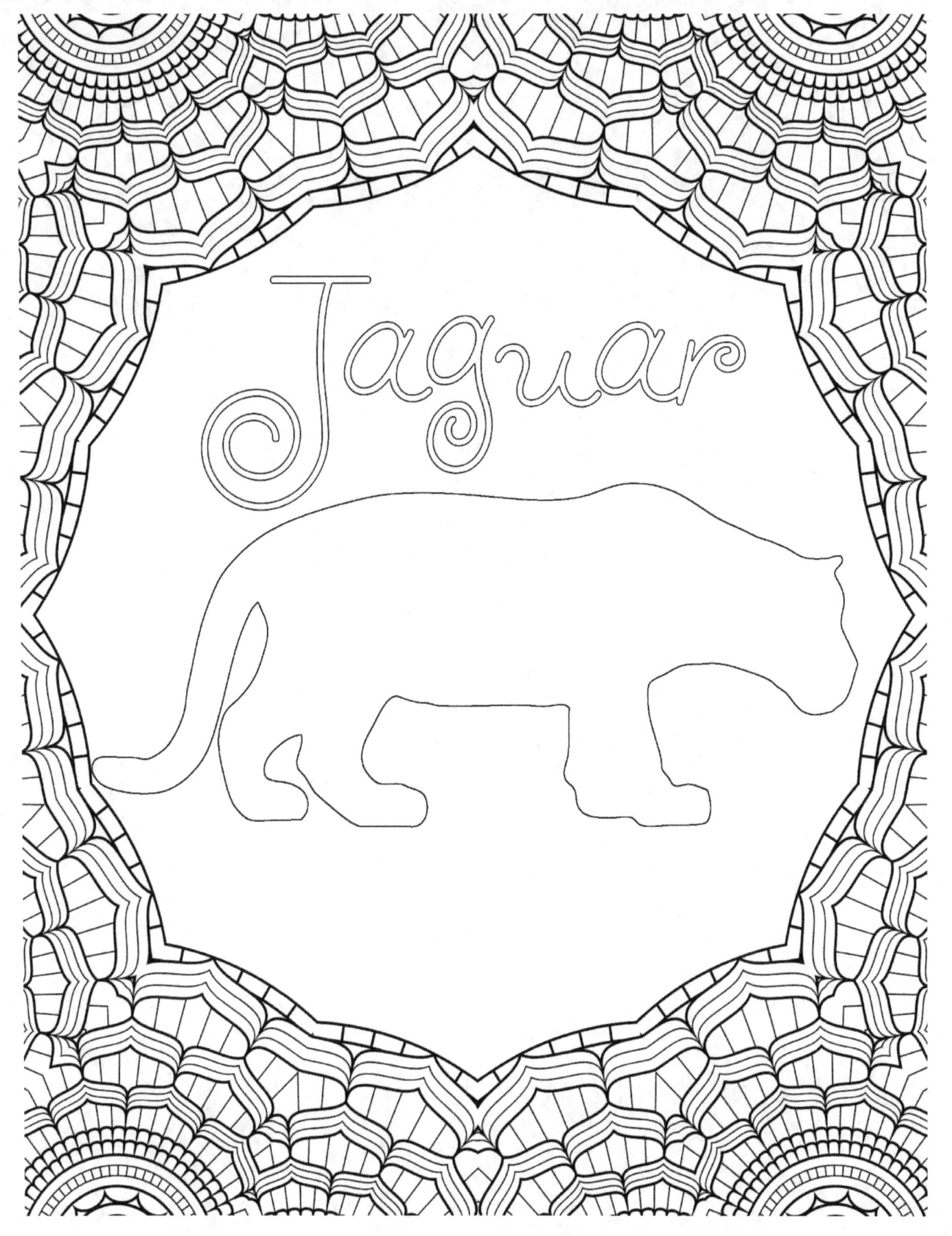

Zebra

Impala

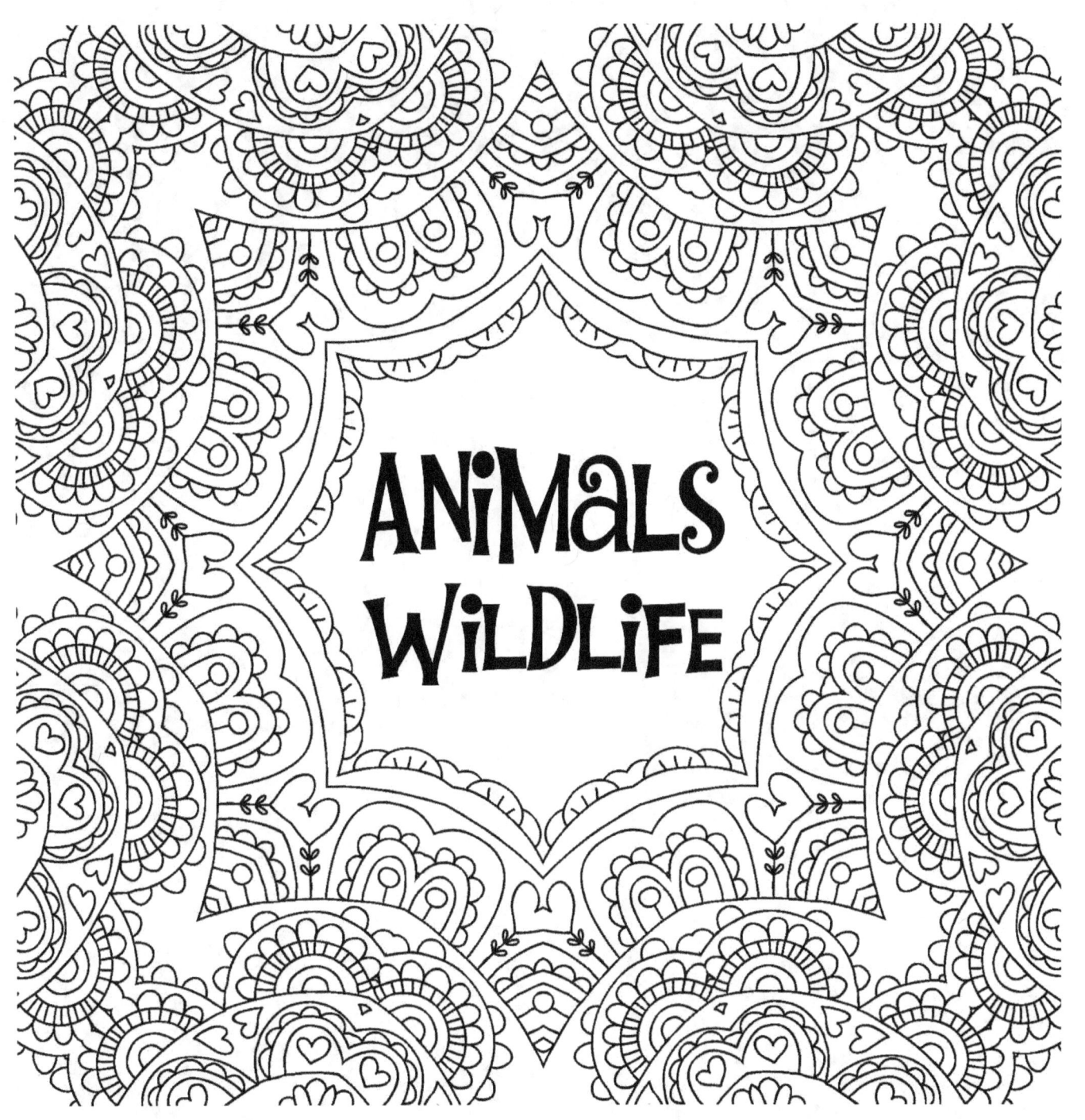

www.ingramcontent.com/pod-product-compliance
Lightning Source LLC
Chambersburg PA
CBHW080324290526
45793CB00006B/1203